Original title:
Berries and Kisses

Copyright © 2025 Creative Arts Management OÜ
All rights reserved.

Author: Alec Donovan
ISBN HARDBACK: 978-1-80586-456-1
ISBN PAPERBACK: 978-1-80586-928-3

## **Passive Pattering of Fruitful Dreams**

Raindrops dance on my head,
A cheerful rhythm, quite widespread.
Mushrooms giggle in the grass,
Feeling ticklish, time does pass.

Pinecones whisper silly tales,
Of adventures with tiny snails.
Each droplet sings a playful tune,
Underneath the lazy moon.

## Dappled Light on Cheeks of Joy

Sunlight plays on cheeks so round,
Fruits tumble down without a sound.
A squirrel chuckles, swipes a treat,
Wobbling off on tiny feet.

Laughter fills the air so bright,
As frogs hop high in pure delight.
Chasing shadows, we all sway,
In this funny, fruity fray.

## Luscious Embrace of Nature's Delight

Lemon drops fall from the skies,
Tickling noses, we all rise.
Honeybees buzz in silly lines,
Juggling nectar, sweeter than vines.

Mango smiles wave from afar,
Cheering on the fruit bazaar.
With each bite, a giggle flows,
As laughter dances in the rows.

## The Aroma of Shared Secrets

Strawberry whispers and cherry winks,
Behind the bushes, it slyly slinks.
A peach rolls down, teasing me,
Laughing, 'catch me, if you can, you see!'

Under the bushes, secrets spill,
As raspberries scheme with playful thrill.
With every scent, a story told,
In this garden, where joy unfolds.

## Love's Nectar in the Ripened Hours

In the garden, fruits abound,
Some are sweet, and some are round.
I took a bite, oh what a mess,
Juice dripped down, a sticky dress.

With every laugh, the moments flew,
A fruit fight started, who knew?
We tossed and splattered with delight,
Eight o'clock turned into a bite!

## Petals and Juices in a Secret Garden

In hidden spots where flowers sway,
We danced around and tried to play.
With petals caught in all our hair,
We giggled loud without a care.

Sipped from cups that overflowed,
Our laughter bloomed as we bestowed.
A splash of color, a dash of cheer,
Who knew this garden held such beer?

## Glimmers of Taste and Tender Touch

A sneaky taste from stolen hands,
We mixed our flavors, made new plans.
The crunch, the pop, a berry zing,
In this mad kitchen, we were kings.

A pinch of joy, a dash of fun,
Our culinary race had just begun.
With laughter rising, pots did clatter,
Who knew that food could lead to chatter?

## Ruby Flavors of Shared Laughter

In every bite, a joke was spun,
With each new flavor, we just had fun.
A biting tease, then sweet romance,
We danced around, began to prance.

With ruby hues that glimmer bright,
Our hearts ignited, oh what a sight!
In every tickle, a taste so bold,
We shared our secrets, stories told.

## **The Taste of Innocence**

Little hands reach for a treat,
Sticky smiles are hard to beat.
Sweets drip down on laughing cheeks,
Joy is found in small techniques.

Chasing critters, what a scene,
Laughter echoes through the green.
Tasting sunshine in the air,
In this realm, there's no despair.

## Flavors of Togetherness

Mixing colors, what a show,
Giggles as we start to throw.
Jam on toes and sticky hair,
Together, we don't have a care.

A splash of juice, a fruity fling,
Silly songs we love to sing.
Tasting magic on my tongue,
Life is vibrant, always young.

### **Velvet Touch of the Harvest**

Softly plucked from nature's hands,
Juicy bites turn into bands.
We dance around with sugary bliss,
Every moment feels like this.

Sweet confessions underneath the trees,
Whispers carried on the breeze.
Every laugh, a gentle nudge,
A feast of fun, we'll never judge.

## Radiance in a Basket

Colorful treasures piled so high,
Wobbling towers—oh my, oh my!
Frolic through the fruity maze,
Every giggle a joyful craze.

In the basket, laughter spills,
Sharing secrets, cheerful thrills.
With each taste, we spin and whir,
Life is sweet, don't you concur?

## The Essence of Warmth and Touch

In the sun, oh how we laugh,
With sticky hands and sweetened gaff.
We dance around, a cheerful mess,
Our giggles tangled, who could guess?

The juice runs down, a crimson flow,
A playful scene, don't steal the show!
We lick our lips, all bold and bright,
As laughter fills the warm twilight.

## Mosaic of Tastes and Trysts.

A patchwork quilt of tastes divine,
With every nibble, hearts align.
A splash of joy, a dash of cheer,
We steal a glance, it's perfectly clear!

With every slice, a frolic spun,
The flavors mix, oh what fun!
A wink exchanged in fruity glee,
Together here, just you and me.

## Sweet Fruits of Affection

Underneath the leafy green,
We share our secrets, not so clean.
A squished delight upon our face,
As sticky fingers set the pace!

Your laughter rings, a sweet refrain,
Two heartbeats dance in joyful chain.
A fruity blunder, and we both sigh,
Oh, what a mess, but we still fly!

## **Juicy Whispers in the Garden**

In the garden where we play,
Each hidden taste wants to sway.
A nibble here, a playful tease,
Leaves us chuckling, hearts at ease.

Whispers sweet like summer air,
With every bite, we show we care.
In this patch, so bold and bright,
We share our dreams in pure delight.

## **Silken Touch of Summer Fruits**

In the garden, a secret delight,
Ripe treasures sparkle, oh what a sight!
A slip and a slide, I giggle and fumble,
Juice drips down, causing me to stumble.

Neighbors peek out, they can't help but stare,
As I tango with fruits, without a care.
A squished one here, a burst of surprise,
Laughter erupts as I wipe my eyes.

## Savoring the Scarlet Embrace

Sweet crimson hugs, all over my face,
Spilling the laughter, oh what a race!
With each tiny burst, my giggles expand,
Sticky fingers wave like they're in a band.

Friends join the fun, it's a fruity affair,
Chasing the drips, without any care.
The ground is a canvas, smeared in delight,
As we feast on the harvest, day turns to night.

## The Taste of Sugar-Laden Dreams

In the twilight glow, dreams taste so sweet,
A pinch of enchantment, my favorite treat.
With a flick of my tongue, the flavors unite,
Dancing and spinning, oh what a night!

Whispers of sugar wrap round with a grin,
Laughter erupts as we dance in a spin.
The stars in the sky, they blink and they wink,
As we lick our spoons and forget time to think.

## **Petals and Plumpness Rejoice**

Today, I stumbled through a garden of cheer,
Petals and plumpness whisper secrets near.
A sneaky little nibble, a giggle escapes,
While bees buzz around, plotting their shapes.

Flavors collide, a raucous delight,
Spinning in circles till we take flight.
With every bright taste, our spirits ascend,
In this silly season, fun knows no end.

## Landscapes of Flavor and Affection

Splash of shades so bright,
Laughter drips like juice,
A squirrel may take flight,
Stealing sweets, of course!

The crunch, the joy, the taste,
Oh, that squishy surprise,
With sunshine interlaced,
And cheeky little pies.

Buzzing bees on the prowl,
Dance upon your cheek,
A giggle—their scowl,
As sticky hands peek!

We weaved a lovely scene,
With bites far too big,
Oh, what could have been,
If only we could dig!

## Beneath the Boughs of Warmth

Underneath the canopy,
Where secrets softly spring,
A bear named Earl—oh me!
Dreams of pudding fling!

The plump ones jump and roll,
Like cheeky little sprites,
With giggles on a stroll,
And bulges that excite.

A little tug, a grimace,
The sticky mess unfolds,
We trade our sweet embrace,
With stories yet untold!

So come, my silly friend,
Let's dance until we burst,
With every twist and bend,
The funny leaves us thirst!

## Revelations in a Patch of Light

In a patch of gold and green,
Where surprises seem to thrive,
A tangle of giggles keen,
And bushes buzz with drive!

The juicy splats we chase,
Like eager little spies,
We've mastered the art of grace,
With juice that flies in pies!

A plucky monkey peeks afar,
With twinkling eyes of glee,
He's swinging from the star,
Searching for the spree!

Be wary of the green hands,
With sticky tales behind,
In this world, no demands,
Only joy defined!

## Constellations of Fruitful Wishes

Up in the sky's embrace,
A harvest of sweet dreams,
We'd twirl and trade our space,
Like sunlight's playful beams!

A red-haired sprite would scold,
For taking one too much,
"Don't be so bold, be told!"
She'd laugh, and start to clutch.

With mischief in our hearts,
We'd run beneath the stars,
Creating funny arts,
With bursting fruit-filled jars!

To wish on juicy stars,
And taste the cosmic glow,
We'll dance on grassy bars,
In nature's great tableau!

## Craving the Taste of Innocent Joy

In the garden where giggles grow,
A sprightly dance, a lovely show.
Plump little treats dangle from the vine,
A teasing game, a twist of the line.

Juicy drops, oh what a tease,
Tickling noses in the gentle breeze.
With every bite, a splash of glee,
Who knew sweetness could also be silly?

Laughter bubbles like soda pop,
As we munch and skip, we just can't stop.
Red-stained cheeks, a glorious mess,
In this frolic, we feel so blessed.

Come, let's chase those playful dreams,
In nature's lap, where joy redeems.
With laughter ringing, time flies by,
Our innocent joy, where all birds fly.

## Echoes of Laughter in Nature's Cradle

Under the sun, where shadows play,
We plot our mischief, come what may.
Whispers of joy in every bush,
Nature's laughter gives our hearts a rush.

Chasing critters and tripping roots,
One silly stumble leads to hoots.
Bright splashes of color, wild and free,
The world's a canvas, just wait and see.

Furry friends join in the fun,
Every moment shines bright like the sun.
In sweet chaos, we find our cheer,
Nature's giggle is loud and clear.

With hands sticky and hearts so light,
Every hiccup feels just right.
In this cradle, time's a jest,
Embracing the mess, we feel so blessed.

## Rich Tastes and Playful Moods

A basket brimming with treats divine,
Shiny delights, enough for ten dine.
The taste of mischief, a bold delight,
Each nibble brings giggles, such fun tonight.

Cheerful games, a sweetened chase,
Sticky fingers and laughter's embrace.
Who knew flavors could dance and swirl,
In this tasty kingdom, hearts twirl.

With every bite, a happy cheer,
Mischief and joy are always near.
Colorful bites, a splatter of fun,
Their cheeky nature makes us run!

In playful chaos, we do confess,
Sweets and laughter, we need no less.
Every moment is ripe with glee,
Together we savor, wild and free.

## Autumn Hues and Heartfelt Glances

Leaves fall like confetti, what a sight,
In golden hues, the day feels bright.
Snickers and smiles, we frolic along,
In nature's playground, we all belong.

Juicy treasures dot the cool ground,
With every step, another giggle's found.
Golden pumpkins with silly grins,
We dance with shadows, where fun begins.

An impish breeze tugs at our hair,
We chase the moment without a care.
Every glance hides a playful spark,
Autumn whispers secrets in the dark.

So let's gather 'round for games so bold,
With heartwarming tales, let the joy unfold.
In this vibrant canvas, life runs wild,
The laughter of nature, forever a child.

## **Whispers of Summer Fruit**

In the garden where we sneak,
Colors dance, the fruits all speak.
Giggles rise with every bite,
Sticky fingers, pure delight.

Underneath the blazing sun,
We play games, we laugh, we run.
With every splash of juice we share,
Laughter echoes, fills the air.

The squirrels watch with hungry eyes,
While we pretend to be the prize.
A fruity feast, not just for them,
We'll take it all, we won't condemn.

As evening falls, we find a seat,
Dancing shadows, oh, so sweet.
In our kingdom of summer cheer,
We'll feast till dawn, the end is near.

## **Sweetness on Our Lips**

A red smudge on your cheek, my dear,
You remind me of a cheeky bear.
With every giggle comes a slip,
Our snack time turns into a trip.

Whipped cream on our noses bright,
Every bite brings a silly fight.
You claim the largest slice for you,
But I know what I'm gonna do!

With every squish and every squall,
We share a joke, we start to brawl.
The laughter bubbles, spills like wine,
In our sweet world, everything's fine.

As daylight fades, we take a stand,
With one last scoop, we're hand in hand.
The flavors mixing on our lips,
This funny dance, we'll never skip.

## Juicy Secrets of Midnight

Under stars with a glint of shine,
We sneak bites from the secret vine.
A midnight snack, oh what a sight,
Whispers echo, hearts feel light.

Your laugh rings out like a sweet tune,
As we dodge beams from the glowing moon.
With sticky fingers, we're off the path,
Chasing shadows, escaping math.

A splash of juice, a glossy sheen,
Daring dreams of being unseen.
The world's a game, we're in control,
With fruity treasures for each roll.

As twilight dances on our cheeks,
We share our secrets, giggles peak.
Under the cover of evening's call,
We find our joy within it all.

## Embrace of the Orchard

In a grove where the humor's ripe,
We quote the trees, we play the type.
With nature's fun, we navigate,
In our secret hideaway, we contemplate.

Plucking fruit while dodging bees,
Hopping around with the greatest ease.
Every stumble turns to a cheer,
In this place filled with flavor and fear.

The wind whispers tales of sweets
While we dance to the nature's beats.
A game of toss, a fruit-filled flight,
With laughter spilling, oh what a sight!

In the orchard's warm embrace we smile,
We'll feast and frolic, stay a while.
For in this fruity, funny place,
We find our joy, our special grace.

## Nectar of the Heart

In the garden where laughter thrives,
Silly smiles bring out surprise,
Juicy bites of cheeky dreams,
Tickling taste buds, bursting seams.

A scoop of fun, a dash of cheer,
Swirling joy that's oh-so-clear,
Puckered lips make random sounds,
Giggles bouncing all around.

Frolicking feet on grass so green,
Each little dance, a playful scene,
Sipping sweetness, feeling free,
What a splash of jubilee!

Heartbeats skip, a merry tune,
Whispers sweet beneath the moon,
When joy is served on silver spoons,
Happiness bursts, like balloons!

## **Silent Sighs Under the Canopy**

Beneath the leaves, where shadows play,
Giggles echo, come what may,
A careless breeze, a playful tease,
Fuzzy secrets rustle, squeeze.

Plump delights hide, oh so sweet,
Spilling joy with every treat,
Whimsical tastes, a jolly jest,
Under the trees, we feel our best.

A blush of color, a twist of fate,
Winking stars may just be late,
Muffled laughs in the thick, warm air,
Surprises loom everywhere.

In our cozy, secret space,
Laughter mingles, sets the pace,
With whispered vows and silly whims,
We craft our joy in tiny gems.

## A Dance of Flavor and Emotion

Waltzing through the fields of glee,
Nibbles call, come dance with me,
Chubby cheeks and silly grins,
Flavors tangle, spin like spins.

Marshmallow clouds and whip of cream,
Frothy giggles in the streams,
Every inch, a twist, a turn,
Craving joy that's hard to spurn.

The rhythm of taste, a joyful sprint,
Crunchy bites, then a happy hint,
A playful bounce, a merry swirl,
Silly whispers, watch them twirl.

In the dance of joy we find,
Cheeky treasures intertwined,
With every step, we leap and shout,
Growing giggles, there's no doubt!

## **Hidden Gardens of Bliss**

In a corner of the bright, warm day,
Cheerful giggles come out to play,
With hints of sweetness, joyful splashes,
Hidden treasures, oh how it clashes!

The greenest leaves hide silly sights,
Where laughter blooms in colorful lights,
A sprinkle here, a dash of that,
Bouncing joy like a playful cat.

Petals whisper, secrets shared,
A feast of fun, a heart that dared,
Rolling laughter, a jolly spree,
In our secret world, we're wild and free.

Each delight leaves a happy mark,
Stumbling through this dreamy park,
With brightened eyes and joyous hearts,
In hidden gardens, laughter starts!

## **Vibrant Hues of an Unspoken Bond**

In a patch of colors bright,
Two friends share a berry bite.
With juice that stains their happy lips,
They giggle through their fruity quips.

One says, 'Is this a fruit affair?
Or just a sweet, hilarious dare?'
They laugh, a playful blush of red,
As crumbs and giggles fill their spread.

Splat! A rogue fruit flies through the air,
Lands in hair with its juicy flair.
Amid the chaos, joy does bloom,
In this circus of colors, fun resumes.

With vibrant hues on every grin,
They make a world where laughs begin.
Each splash of color tells a tale,
Of silliness that will never pale.

## Nectar Laced with Sweet Wishes

A sunlit scene of sticky dreams,
Two pals giggle with syrupy beams.
'It's magic!' one says with glee so bright,
While tasting joy in every bite.

They toast with cups of nectar pure,
A friendship sweet that's meant to endure.
With every sip, they make a wish,
For more of this laughter and fruity swish.

One spills the drink right on their shoe,
While the other laughs, 'I think that's new!'
They dance around, a sticky spree,
In a world where fun is the only decree.

The nectar glistens like sunshine's glow,
Each shared sip ignites the show.
In a whirl of flavors, joy they blend,
In this zany joyride, there's no end.

## Glints of Joy in the Soft Terrain

In a meadow where laughter reigns,
Two giggling hearts embrace the gains.
They skip through grasses, soft and green,
Collecting chuckles, it's quite the scene.

One stumbles, sends a tangle of vines,
While the other bursts into silly rhymes.
As the sunlight dapples their feet,
Their laughter echoes, oh so sweet!

They pick the fluffiest clouds of fluff,
Wipe off the mud—oh, isn't this tough?
In this garden, with smiles so wide,
Even the daisies bloom with pride.

With every step, they leap and bound,
In this soft terrain, pure joy is found.
Like little sprites in a playful dream,
Their friendship sparkles, a vibrant gleam.

## A Garden of Vibrant Sentiments

In a garden bursting with silly schemes,
Two friends dig deep into their dreams.
They plant seeds of laughter with care,
Unfurling giggles in the sunny air.

Among the blooms, they share tall tales,
Of purple penguins and singing snails.
Each flower nods as if to say,
'What a wild and whimsical day!'

They sprinkle cheer like magic dust,
Creating joy that's filled with trust.
With clumsy hands, they toss confetti,
In this patch of laughter, everything's ready!

As the sun sets, they take a seat,
Surrounded by jokes—a berry sweet treat.
In this garden, love takes flight,
With vibrant sentiments to ignite the night.

## Love's Edible Serenade

In a garden, secrets hum,
Tiny fruits of laughter come.
Chubby cheeks in sunlit cheer,
Giggles roll, you lend an ear.

Silly faces, juice on chins,
We both dance while the laughter spins.
With playful bites, we claim our snacks,
In silly games, there are no hacks.

Sticky fingers, sweetened bliss,
Every nibble brings a twist.
A plump surprise, oh what a treat,
Your laughter makes my heart skip beat.

As flavors swirl, our smiles grow,
Endless joy in a fruit-filled show.
With each bite, a silly delight,
Our hearts burst forth in silly flight.

## **Wild Echoes of Delight**

A romp through vines, we race and play,
Ripe wonders make us shout hooray.
With cheeky grins, we scoop and munch,
Chasing shadows, missing lunch.

Juicy dribbles stain our clothes,
Who knew fun would come in rows?
A giggle fest, as we collide,
In a forest's laughter, we abide.

Sunlight glimmers, shadows tease,
Wild antics danced upon the breeze.
With nature's bounty all around,
In silly antics, joy is found.

Chomp and giggle, slip and slide,
In the wild, we take our stride.
Each little laugh, a colorful dance,
With every bite, we spin and prance.

## Heartfelt Harvest

In the orchard, playful scoops,
Gathering joy like fruit-crazed troops.
With laughter ringing in the air,
Our silly contest, without a care.

Pockets stuffed with treasures bright,
Squeezed together, love takes flight.
Grins explode like berries crushed,
In every moment, hearts are hushed.

A plump surprise, you take a bite,
Juice drips down; oh what a sight!
In sticky mess, our faces beam,
Bonding through a tasty dream.

Every taste a wink or jest,
In this bounty, we are blessed.
Heralding laughter with every feast,
From nature's heart, our joys released.

## **Moonlit Nibbles**

Under stars, we softly creep,
Carrying spoons, while others sleep.
Nibbling goodies we have found,
In midnight antics, laughter's bound.

With cheeks aglow from sweets we share,
Whispers drift upon the air.
Each little bite, a story spun,
In moonlit mischief, we have fun.

Here's a pinch, and here's a taste,
No time for rules, let's make haste.
A tangle of laughter in every scoop,
In the night's embrace, we form a loop.

Joyful echoes, silly dreams,
In hidden treats, hear laughter's schemes.
Our secret world beneath the light,
A scrumptious tale, both fun and bright.

## Fragrant Laughter in the Garden

In a patch of bright delight,
Red and round, they'd dance in light.
A squirrel spies with cheeky glee,
As they roll down, wild and free.

A ladybug joins the fun,
Winks at them, oh what a run!
They giggle, bounce from leaf to leaf,
Nature's laughter, pure, no grief.

Sunshine paints a playful scene,
As they hop, they burst with sheen.
A playful breeze will shake it right,
And turn their blush into a flight.

In the garden, laughter flows,
With each roll, big smiles grow.
A feast of sweetness in the sun,
Nature's giggles, oh what fun!

## Crimson Stains of Desire

A squished delight upon my chin,
Oh my, where to even begin?
With every bite, a splash so red,
It drips and splatters, oh what dread!

A crunchy snack that takes a turn,
The juice drips down, igniting burn.
My shirt, a canvas, now a mess,
What laughter now, I must confess!

With sticky fingers and a grin,
I wonder how these games begin.
A swipe of fruit across my face,
This playful chase, a silly race!

Crimson stains, a badge of pride,
In this chaos, I can't hide.
With giggles ringing in the air,
It's all for fun, without a care!

## Sunlit Juiciness

In the sun, a sweet parade,
Round and shiny, no charade.
They roll and tumble, catching rays,
With giggles bright through summer days.

A cheeky bird begins to peck,
Sipping juice from every speck.
With every bite, a joyful song,
Nature hums, we sing along.

One slippery drop goes astray,
And makes its way to where I play.
My laughter rings, the sun shall see,
How juicy fun can always be!

With friends around, the day is grand,
We share the sweetness, hand in hand.
With every laugh and playful jest,
We feast on sunshine, blissfully blessed.

## Tender Moments in the Meadow

In a meadow green and wide,
Little gems, they softly glide.
With every step, a giggle bursts,
A frolic here quenches all thirsts.

A butterfly, with flapping grace,
Twirls around to join our race.
They sneak and peek, a playful tease,
While we all tumble with such ease.

Tracing trails of juice and fun,
Underneath the bright warm sun.
With every laugh, a memory grows,
In tender moments, sweetness flows.

So here we dance, in simple cheer,
With tiny gems, our hearts draw near.
In the meadow, where laughs resound,
These silly days, forever found.

## The Sweet Serenade of Nature's Hand

In the garden, laughter blooms,
With red delights and fruity looms.
Fingers sticky, running free,
Nature's joy, such glee to see!

Nature's mischief on the vine,
Taste the sun, it's quite divine.
Giggles float on breezy air,
As we feast without a care!

Juicy drips and fruity smears,
Sharing laughter, shedding tears.
Every bite a silly dance,
In this tasty, sunny trance!

So let the sweetness paint the day,
With nature's tricks in bright display.
Laughter echoes, pure delight,
In the garden, hearts take flight!

## Boundary Lines of Cream and Fruit

Splatters of cream on my nose,
A playful smile, the chaos grows.
Dancing spoons in a silly duel,
Everyone's giggling, it's the golden rule!

From cup to cheek, a wild chase,
Strawberry smudges all over the place.
Sweet explosions in every spoon,
A dessert debate beneath the moon!

Mischief flows, we laugh and tease,
Taste buds tango with such ease.
A scoop here, a scoop there,
Creamy chaos fills the air!

The lines are blurred in fruity delight,
Oops! My dessert took flight!
With every laugh, the joy's multiplied,
In this creamy fray, we take pride!

## **Warmth Carried in Juicy Currents**

Golden rays and wild shouts,
Sticky fingers, joyful bouts.
Taking chances with every bite,
Catching sweetness, pure delight!

Sunshine glows on cheeky smiles,
Tasting joy in fruity piles.
With every splash, the laughter grows,
Bursting flavors steal the show!

Rolling tastes down grassy hills,
Chasing flavors, feeling thrills.
Friends unite in a juicy fight,
Every moment feels so right!

So let the juice flow, oh so wide,
With giggles and smiles as our guide.
In this nectar-filled parade,
Heartfelt warmth is truly made!

# An Unwritten Poem of Harvested Joy

In fields of joy, we gather round,
Whispers of fruit, a silly sound.
Underneath the sun's warm glow,
Laughter ripens, love will grow!

Nature's bounty dressed in glee,
A playful bite, come share with me!
Giggles echo 'neath the trees,
Sweetness dancing in the breeze!

With every taste, a memory flies,
Caught mid-air, beneath blue skies.
The harvest sings a fun-filled tune,
An unwritten recipe, joy in bloom!

So frolic here, sweet and bold,
In this poem, let love unfold.
With playful jests and fruity cheer,
Harvested moments, hold them dear!

## Symphony of Delicate Touches

In a garden where giggles grow,
Tiny delights put on quite a show.
Nibbles that blush and tease the tongue,
A fruit parade, where laughter's sung.

Every splash of color, quite absurd,
Like paint splattered by a cheeky bird.
They dance upon pancakes, sashay on toast,
Devouring them all, we laugh the most.

Whimsical tastes that cause a cheer,
Each squishy pop, brings joy and beer.
With each playful munch, we skip and twirl,
In this fruity realm, our laughter's a whirl.

Silly concoctions made just for fun,
A fruity explosion, oh what a run!
With smiles as sweet as the treats we find,
In this playful feast, we're all so blind.

**The Color of Happiness in Every Bite**

A burst of zest upon my plate,
Round like smiles, they dance in fate.
They jive and wiggle, a fruity tease,
Tickling taste buds, they aim to please.

Like candy sprinkles on a warm cake,
They giggle and hum, oh what a quake!
Bright as sunshine, wild and free,
Taste sensations that bring glee, oh me!

Each pop and crunch, a ticklish glee,
They glisten and glimmer, just like me.
In every mouthful, joy takes flight,
A rainbow of flavors, pure delight.

As we feast on giggles and winks alike,
With fruity treasures, we strike a spike.
Laughing together, a sweetened cheer,
These joyful bites draw us all near.

## **Elixirs of Affection in the Wild**

In the forest where whimsy flies,
Fragrant treats beneath the skies.
A dainty pluck brings forth a grin,
Nature's pun that draws us in.

Each little orb, a jest or two,
Whispering secrets, just me and you.
Squeezed on desserts, they paint the air,
Like silly hats that we all wear.

With each delightful, soggy squirt,
A mischievous face and a playful flirt.
Juicy tricks played on every plate,
A scrumptious joke, oh isn't that great?

From picnic baskets to froggy dives,
These flavors dance and keep us alive.
In nature's jest, our spirits soar,
A wild smirk, who could ask for more?

## The Rhythms of Fruity Emotions

Oh, the tunes of the tart and sweet,
Funky flavors, tapping our feet.
A jam session inside the bowl,
Sassy notes that swell and roll.

They jingle and jive in our tummies,
Bouncing about like little bunnies.
With every bite, the laughter swells,
As stories unfold, and mischief dwells.

Their colors explode, like confetti flair,
A fruit fiesta beyond compare.
As the day breaks with joy anew,
We frolic and feast, just me and you.

Stumbling through moments, silly and bright,
Chasing each giggle with pure delight.
In fruity rhythms, we find our song,
With laughter and love, we can't go wrong.

## Sunlit Murmurs of the Heart

In a garden bright where the laughter springs,
A dance of colors, joyfully flings.
Tiny fruits giggle, teasing my taste,
While butterflies waltz, no moment to waste.

With every splash of sweet, sticky jam,
I find myself grinning like a silly lamb.
The sun takes a sip from the dew on the vine,
While I'm stuck in a grin, completely divine.

Who knew a fruit could take on a laugh,
Ripe with mischief, it sketches a path.
Every plump hug, a wink in disguise,
Sparking my heart, as it twirls and it flies.

So here's to the moments, light and absurd,
When joy is a whisper, far more than a word.
In the sun's warm embrace, life's a fun little art,
As I munch on the treasures that tickle my heart.

## Embers of Passion in Nature's Bowl

In the forest's embrace where the laughter grows,
Nature's red wonders bloom, striking a pose.
They twirl on the branches, a shy little crew,
Whispering secrets, oh what a view!

Each scoop from the bowl, a zany surprise,
A splatter of joy that tickles the skies.
The taste is a giggle, a sweet little jest,
While squirrels roll laughter, they know who is best.

The mix of the flavors, so wild and so free,
Makes me laugh wildly, near a buzzing bee.
With veggies and fruits in a tumble and toss,
I swear this mishap is worth all the gloss!

So grab a big spoon and join in the fun,
The laughter and sweetness in life can't be done.
Let's stir up our dreams in this nature-made bowl,
And savor the joy that tickles the soul!

## The Sweetness of Forgotten Lullabies

Once upon a time, in a sweet little grove,
Dreams hummed softly, dressed in green clove.
Nostalgia tickles like a warm summer rain,
As memories dance, I can't help but feign.

The flavors of youth, in a syrupy swirl,
Remind me of giggles, giving my heart a twirl.
With each splash of flavor, I find myself lost,
In a world where sweetness is worth any cost.

Oh the jests of the past, like a tune in the breeze,
Made me chuckle softly, brought me to my knees.
With laughter like nectar, my heart starts to bloom,
In the symphony of tastes, I sweep all the gloom.

So let's toast to the echoes of laughter and cheer,
To days filled with sweetness, come grab me a beer!
For in this rhythm of jests wrapped in rhyme,
I'll sing out the joys, oh what a grand time!

## Nature's Caress Beneath a Sky

Underneath the wide expanse where giggles arise,
Nature's flirtations draw laughs from the skies.
Each little nibble is a wink from the earth,
As butterflies frolic, they party with mirth.

The trees wear green hats, waving hello,
While hops and skips merge in a whimsical flow.
Every juicy morsel sparks shrieks of delight,
As daylight dances on, from morning to night.

Clouds dress in patches, like cakes on a stand,
With raindrops like sprinkles, oh isn't it grand?
The sun's cheeky rays beam down with a grin,
Spreading joy as the cycle of laughter begins.

So gather your pals, let's spin and we'll sway,
Nature's our playground, let's play every day.
For in every giggle, a story unfolds,
In a symphony of joy, life's sweetness molds.

## **The Essence of Joy on the Tongue**

A plump little treasure, round and bright,
It winks at me in morning light.
I take a nibble, oh such a treat,
My taste buds dance, it's a tasty feat.

From crimson sweet to purple tart,
Each joyful burst, a foodie art.
I'm giggling now, who needs a feast?
Just this small round, I am a beast!

With juice that splatters, shirts run wild,
Oh no! I've stained like a reckless child.
But laughter rings, and that's the plan,
With flavor fun, I'm in joyful land.

A silly smile, I can't resist,
It's snack time bliss, oh how I've missed!
Each nibble's magic, laughter stirred,
Life's little prank, it's absurd!

## Sips of Silver Sunshine in Every Bite

A sip of sweet, the sunlight spills,
Each tiny drop gives countless thrills.
I raise my glass, a toast up high,
To fruity days, oh my, oh my!

With frothy frolic, bubbles rise,
This sparkly juice, a fun surprise.
I tap my glass, a clink, a cheer,
For juice-filled joy, we draw so near!

My cheeks are rosy, laughter flows,
With every sip, my giggle grows.
A splash of zing, oh what a show,
A thimbleful makes our joy tow!

So here we laugh, we drink and play,
In fruity turns, we'll sway all day.
With smiles aglow, as sweet as pie,
We sip our cheer and let joy fly!

## The Scented Promise in Every Shade

Oh look at colors, vibrant, bold,
Each little fruit, a tale retold.
From rosy blush to deepest blue,
This fruity magic, a joyous hue!

A sniff, a swirl, what joy I smell,
In every shade, a story to tell.
Beware the tang! It might surprise,
A zesty kick, oh me, oh my!

They dance on plates, a festive sight,
A rainbow feast, oh pure delight.
With pokes and prods, I take my pick,
The funny shapes just do their trick!

So roll me round, these colors bold,
In laughter's grip, I'll never fold.
From sweet to sour, I laugh and play,
Such scented promises every day!

## Delicate Flavors and Hidden Thorns

Oh gentle bites, with a pinch of zest,
Each tiny taste is quite the quest.
But beware, my friend, the little prick,
A cheeky sneak can do the trick!

With careful nibbles, I take a chance,
In flavors' game, we cheekily dance.
Oh such delight, with laughter shared,
Yet on my fingers, a thorn is bared.

The giggles rise as munching grows,
Each delighted sigh, the fun just flows.
I playfully wiggle, oh what a fuss,
In every bite, joy's a must!

So join my game, let's share this glee,
In every dainty, we'll just be free.
With delicate whimsy and giggling glee,
Life's a laughter, won't you see?

## Lush Secrets of the Vine

In the garden, secrets bloom,
A dance of colors, a sweet perfume.
Giggles hide behind bright hues,
Where squishy treasures play peek-a-boo.

Little hands reach for delight,
Sticky fingers, oh what a sight!
Nature's treasure, a playful tease,
Wink at the world, if you please.

Buzzing bees humming a tune,
Cheeky critters joining the swoon.
Under the leaves, laughter's a must,
Who knew a plant could spark such trust?

Whispers of joy, under the sun,
Life in the garden is pure fun.
Strawberry stains on a cheeky grin,
This fruity adventure is just the beginning.

**Sunkissed Smiles and Nectar**

Sun-warmed flutters, sweet and bright,
Chasing the bees, oh what a sight!
With each sip, the giggles grow,
Merry moments put on a show.

Behold the sweetness, caught in a jar,
A taste of joy, oh how bizarre!
Dribbles down chins, laughter sings,
Sticky situations, oh the joys it brings!

Mischief brews with a fruity flair,
Sunkissed cheeks, no one can compare.
With every bite, a chuckle erupts,
Who knew nature's candy could come with hiccups?

Laughter echoes, fluttering by,
Wandering wonders beneath the sky.
Each drop of nectar, a ticklish tease,
In this merry garden, we dance with ease.

## Cherry-Picked Affections

In the orchard, love's in the air,
With each fruit, a quirky dare.
Reaching high for the ripest prize,
Under the branches, endless surprise.

Each round scoop is quite an art,
Fruits that tangle with the heart.
A smudge of red upon the nose,
Laughter spills as sweetness flows.

Tales of mischief, take their flight,
Catch a giggle in the moonlight.
Bouncing smiles, sweetness in tow,
Who knew affection could take this flow?

Every twinkle is a secret told,
In this fruity fiesta, brave and bold.
Cherry-picked quips, a feast of cheer,
With every bite, come gather near!

## **Petals and Pluck**

Among the petals, charm is found,
A giggle here, a hiccup sound.
With each step, the mischief brews,
Nature's jokes in bright reviews.

Plucking joy from every sprout,
With laughter ringing all about.
Nudging blossoms, here and there,
Sweet giggles dance upon the air.

Bouncing blooms like silly hats,
Each twist and turn, a playful chat.
A garden party, come join the fun,
With every smile, the clock can't run!

So frolic through this patch of glee,
With petals around, just you and me.
Laughter echoes with every clue,
A joyful romp in a world so new.

## The Fruitful Ballet of Heartstrings

In a garden where giggles grow,
The dance of sweet laughter flows.
Tiny twirls and playful hops,
All in rhythm, no one stops.

Sticky fingers, a fruity fight,
Chasing shadows, pure delight.
Under the sun, we wear our hats,
Giggles burst like bouncing sprats.

The waltz of flavors surprises me,
Sipping sunshine, wild and free.
Every spin, a burst of glee,
Who knew fruit could be this silly?

So, let's tango with nature's whims,
Twinkling eyes and joyful hymns.
With every bite, a surprising twist,
In this dance, we simply can't resist.

## **Succulent Promises in the Air**

Whispers of sweetness float around,
Promises where happiness is found.
A game of peek-a-boo with the sun,
Laughter's echo, oh what fun!

Juicy secrets hidden below,
Tickle fights with giggles in tow.
In each corner, surprises hide,
A scrumptious jest, oh what a ride!

Bouncing cheeks, a vibrant scene,
Winks exchanged, laughter keen.
Under the arch of summer skies,
The air is thick with tasty lies.

In this world of fruity dreams,
Every smile bursts at the seams.
Silly puns and bright confessions,
Harvesting joy in all its sessions.

## A Dance of Juicy Delights

Round and round, we leap and glide,
With fruity flavors as our guide.
A hop, a skip, a knack for fun,
In this juicy whirl, we twirl as one.

Mischief bubbles in the air,
Bright colors make a vibrant pair.
With every giggle, we chime in tune,
Dancing under the playful moon.

Sticky sweets upon our cheeks,
A ballet of flavors, oh so unique.
Twists and turns on grassy floors,
Laughter spills from open doors.

Sweetened air, a playful tease,
In this whirl, we catch the breeze.
Each moment ripe with silly spice,
Dancing through life, oh, how nice!

## Harvesting the Flavors of Love

With a wink and a loving grin,
We gather dreams, let the fun begin.
Flavors bursting, a merry feast,\nIn our hearts, joy is released.

Pitter-patter of tiny feet,
As we stumble, our giggles meet.
In this orchard, hearts take flight,
Chasing dreams beneath starlight.

Each pluck from the trees above,
Wraps us in a cloak of love.
Laughter echoes through the glen,
A playful dance time and again.

Tickling whimsies, a merry chase,
In the arms of joy, we find our place.
Every moment a cherished cheer,
Harvesting laughter that draws us near.

## Tangy Echoes of Embraced Souls

In the orchard where laughter grows,
Juicy bits hang like fruity prose.
Tickled by whispers, giggles ensue,
Caught in a splash of the morning dew.

Silly steps on a zesty spree,
Chasing the sweetness, oh can't you see?
A twist and a turn, we dance with glee,
Like two jumbled flavors in a cup of tea.

With each silly smudge, we paint the day,
Spittle and chuckles, come what may.
Beneath the vibrant sun's warm embrace,
We drip with joy, no one can replace.

The fruit of our wanderings, wild and free,
In each tart moment, you and me.
Echoes of laughter, ripe and untamed,
Oh, how the fun of our frolics is famed!

## Sweet Delights on Lips of Thyme

Whisked away on a fragrant breeze,
Smiles pop like bubbles, and laughter frees.
Mouth full of mischief and a hint of zest,
Playing with flavors, we outsmart the rest.

In a twisting dance of fumbled delight,
A plummet of sweetness into the night.
With a pinch of the herb, oh what a ride,
Chasing our dreams with cheeks open wide.

Dainty delights sneak upon our cheek,
As we nibble and giggle, not a moment meek.
The mystery thickens, who took a bite?
Our spirited feast lasts far into night.

Between gags of joy, we trip and burst,
With every weird flavor, oh how we thirst!
Solid hearts made of sugary charm,
Wrapped in a hug, tasting-love warm.

## Warmth of the Sun's Blush

The sun drops a wink, sprinkled with rays,
Chasing our worries, brightening our days.
Laughter ignites in the air like spritz,
As we tumble and roll in frivolous fits.

Tickled by warmth that paints the sky,
We share smirks and chuckles while passing by.
Sunbeams entwined with playful delight,
Radiant moments that bounce into sight.

With shimmering glances, we glint and glow,
In the bright patch of laughter, joy flows so slow.
Who knew fun fruit could pack such a punch?
A slip of the tongue in a zest-filled brunch!

As shadows take flight, we rise with the stars,
Kisses of sun on our playful memoirs.
Wrapped in the warmth of erupting giggles,
Life feels so sweet with all of its wiggles!

## **Tender Fruits Beneath Moonlit Skies**

Under the gaze of the silvery glow,
We play in the garden, taking it slow.
Whispers of mischief float in the night,
With double entendres, we're a curious sight.

A pluck of the night, we launch into fits,
Each shadow undulating with cheeky wits.
Innocent giggles, how daring the dance,
As we leap through the moonbeams, lost in a trance.

Fruits hanging low, a comical tease,
We tumble together with giggling ease.
Laughter and sweetness wrap round like a tape,
Silliness reigns in this night's long escape.

With each juicy bite, a tongue-tied affair,
The night's vibrant whispers swirl in our hair.
In this chaos of sweetness, we find our tune,
Beneath the moon's gaze and the playful balloon!

## **Juices Dripping with Memories**

Red stains on a shirt, oh what a sight,
Laughing as we clean, feels just so right.
Sticky fingers clutching a sugary prize,
What a way to treasure those sweet, silly skies.

Sunshine caught in jars, we sip with glee,
Each gulp's a trip down our memory spree.
Old tales and giggles bubble in each sip,
An echo of laughter, a berry-stained trip.

## Sweets Between the Leaves

Under leafy tunnels where giggles abound,
We search for treasure on the forgotten ground.
A hidden stash of sweetness we find,
Laughter ignites as we nibble and unwind.

The honeyed nectar drips down our chin,
A sticky dilemma, yet we can't help but grin.
Hands raised in triumph, we've conquered the globe,
In our candy-coated leafy robe.

**Fragile Moments on a Summer's Breath**

Butterflies dance while we chase with delight,
But the snack we crafted, takes off in flight.
A wiggly worm leaps at my best friend's nose,
Amidst summer chaos, our laughter only grows.

Soft petals quiver, as we take a bite,
Silly faces made, oh what a fright!
With giggles and crumbs all over the place,
Those fragile moments, we'll never erase.

## **Enchanted Fruit of the Soul**

In a secret garden where silly dreams dwell,
Each fruit tells a story, oh, can you tell?
Magic in every splash, yellow, red, and blue,
The taste of the whimsical, that's just for you.

With every mischievous spin, the flavors collide,
Like traditions of old where the giggles abide.
Silly concoctions with laughter at heart,
In this enchanted realm, we each play our part.

## Morning Dew and Sugar Plum Dreams

In the morning's light, oh so bright,
A drop of joy takes its flight.
It dances on leaves, like giggling kids,
Chasing the sun, while the world still bids.

With whispers of sweetness, it calls my name,
A sugar rush, an animated game.
I think I'm in love with this playful dew,
But I can't tell the ground, or it'll just stew!

Still, on my toast, I spread the delight,
A little too much? Well, that's alright!
With every bite, I chuckle and grin,
As crumbs of laughter tumble right in.

So here's to mornings, all bright and new,
Where giggles and drips are the morning brew.
Dance with your spread, don't trip on the way,
For laughter's the breakfast we all crave today.

**Soft Caresses of Nature**

Tickle my toes with the grass so green,
Nature's touch is quite the scene.
A butterfly flutters, whispers a tease,
As I swat at the air like I'm swatting at bees.

The wind sings a song, a humorous tune,
Slapping my cheeks, oh, who'd have thought?
As flowers around me join in the jest,
Each bloom full of giggles, nature's best dressed!

I tripped on a root, made quite the display,
The squirrels burst out laughing, hurrah for the day!
I rolled on the ground, gave it a kiss,
And even the worms thought, "This moment's pure bliss!"

So come join the fun, get lost in the trees,
Nature's a stand-up show, if you please.
With every little blunder and every new sound,
Soft touches of laughter wrap us all 'round.

## A Symphony of Sweet Surprises

In the orchard's embrace, we gather each fruit,
Unexpected bursts of sweetness to loot.
A dance in the breeze, a slapstick delight,
As I pluck a peach and it takes off in flight!

With cherries that wink and plums that do flip,
I'm caught in a whirlwind, a fruity love trip.
The grapes start to giggle, the apples just sigh,
But I'll catch that juicy laugh, oh me, oh my!

Each harvest's a jest from the earth's playful hand,
It's a banquet of chuckles, oh isn't it grand?
Fruits of all colors, they tumble with glee,
Every morsel whispers, "Come share this with me!"

So gather your friends, let the laughter take flight,
In this symphony sweet, let's play through the night.
With juicy adventures that spark every smile,
I'll savor these moments, stay a while.

## **Fruits of the Heart**

In the garden of giggles, my heart starts to bloom,
With whispers of sweetness, dispelling all gloom.
A strawberry blush, a raspberry grin,
I swear this love is due to the spin!

With bananas that chuckle and orange zest twists,
I reach for the fruit, I can't resist.
A bowl full of whimsy, each bite is a jest,
As the grapes join the party, they're simply the best!

But wait, what is this? A banana peel?
I slip and I laugh, what a crazy meal!
The fruit's all around, making mischief with cheer,
As I tumble and giggle, it's perfectly clear.

So come celebrate, let your heart feel the fun,
With laughter and love, and the warm morning sun.
In this fruity adventure, joy finds its start,
A delightfully silly, sweet fruit of the heart.

www.ingramcontent.com/pod-product-compliance
Lightning Source LLC
Chambersburg PA
CBHW070321120526
44590CB00017B/2772